Magic Of The Magi

Eliphas Levi

Kessinger Publishing's Rare Reprints

Thousands of Scarce and Hard-to-Find Books on These and other Subjects!

- Americana
- Ancient Mysteries
- Animals
- Anthropology
- Architecture
- Arts
- Astrology
- Bibliographies
- Biographies & Memoirs
- Body, Mind & Spirit
- Business & Investing
- Children & Young Adult
- Collectibles
- Comparative Religions
- Crafts & Hobbies
- Earth Sciences
- Education
- Ephemera
- Fiction
- Folklore
- Geography
- Health & Diet
- History
- Hobbies & Leisure
- Humor
- Illustrated Books
- Language & Culture
- Law
- Life Sciences

- Literature
- Medicine & Pharmacy
- Metaphysical
- Music
- Mystery & Crime
- Mythology
- Natural History
- Outdoor & Nature
- Philosophy
- Poetry
- Political Science
- Science
- Psychiatry & Psychology
- Reference
- Religion & Spiritualism
- Rhetoric
- Sacred Books
- Science Fiction
- Science & Technology
- Self-Help
- Social Sciences
- Symbolism
- Theatre & Drama
- Theology
- Travel & Explorations
- War & Military
- Women
- Yoga
- *Plus Much More!*

We kindly invite you to view our catalog list at:
http://www.kessinger.net

CHAPTER II

MAGIC OF THE MAGI

expounder of mysteries

IT is within probability that Zoroaster is a symbolical name, like that of Thoth or Hermes. According to Eudoxus and Aristotle, he flourished 6000 years before the birth of Plato, but others say that he antedated the siege of Troy by about 500 years. He is sometimes represented as a king of the Bactrians, but the existence of two or three distinct Zoroasters is also one of the speculations.[1] Eudoxus and Aristotle alone would seem to have realised that his personality was magical, and this is why they have placed the Kabalistic epoch of an entire world between the birth of his doctrine and the theurgic reign of Platonic philosophy. As a fact, there are two Zoroasters, that is to say, two expounders of mysteries, one being the son of Ormuzd and the founder of an enlightened instruction, the other being the son of Ahriman and the author of a profanatory unveiling of truth. Zoroaster is the incarnate word of the Chaldeans, the Medes and the Persians ; his legend reads like a prophecy concerning that of Christ, and hence it must be assumed that he had also his Anti-Christ, in accordance with the magical law of universal equilibrium.

To the false Zoroaster must be referred the cultus of material fire and that impious doctrine of divine

---

[1] As such it is old, and a monograph on the subject is included by Jacob Bryant in his *Analysis of Antient Mythology*, vol. ii. p. 38 *et seq.* Following the authorities of his period, and especially Huetius, he says that " they have supposed a Zoroaster, wherever there was a Zoroastrian : that is, wherever the religion of the Magi was adopted, or revived." The two Zoroasters of Lévi represent two principles of religious philosophy.

dualism which produced at a later period the monstrous Gnosis of Manes and the false principles of spurious Masonry. The Zoroaster in question was the father of that materialised Magic which led to the massacre of the Magi and brought their true doctrine at first into proscription and then oblivion. Ever inspired by the spirit of truth, the Church was compelled to condemn—under the names of Magic, Manicheanism, Illuminism and Masonry—all that was in kinship, remote or approximate, with the primitive profanation of the mysteries. One signal example is the history of the Knights Templar, which has been misunderstood to this day.

The doctrines of the true Zoroaster are identical with those of pure Kabalism, and his conceptions of divinity differ in no wise from those of the fathers of the Church. It is the names only that vary; for example, the triad of Zoroaster is the Trinity of Christian teaching, and when he postulates that Triad as subsisting without diminution or division in each of its units, he is expressing in another manner that which is understood by our theologians as the circumincession of the Divine Persons. In his multiplication of the Triad by itself, Zoroaster arrives at the absolute reason of the number 9 and the universal key of all numbers and forms. But those whom we term the three Divine Persons, are called the three depths by Zoroaster. The first, or that of the Father, is the source of faith; the second, being that of the Word, is the well of truth; while the third, or creative action, is the font of love. To check what is here advanced, the reader may consult the commentary of Psellus on the doctrine of the ancient Assyrians: it may be found in the work of Franciscus Patricius on *Philosophical Magic*, p. 24 of the Hamburg edition, which appeared in 1593.

Zoroaster established the celestial hierarchy and all the harmonies of Nature on his scale of nine degrees. He explains by means of the triad whatsoever emanates from the idea and by the tetrad all that belongs to form, thus arriving at the number 7 as the type of creation. Here ends the first initiation and the scholastic hypotheses begin; numbers are personified and ideas pass into emblems, which at a later period become idols. The Synoches, the Teletarchæ and the Fathers, ministers of the triple Hecate; the three Amilictes and the threefold visage of Hypezocos—all these intervene; the angels follow in their order, the demons and lastly human souls. The stars are images and reflections of intellectual splendours; the material sun is an emblem of the sun of truth, which itself is a shadow of that first source whence all glory springs. This is why the disciples of Zoroaster saluted the rising day and so passed as sun-worshippers among barbarians.

Such were the doctrines of the Magi, but they were the possessors in addition of secrets which gave them mastery over the occult powers of Nature. The sum of these secrets might be termed transcendental pyrotechny, for it was intimately related to the deep knowledge of fire and its ruling. It is certain that the Magi were not only familiar with electricity but were able to generate and direct it in ways that are now unknown. Numa, who studied their rites and was initiated into their mysteries, possessed, according to Lucius Pison, the art of producing and controlling the lightning. This sacerdotal secret, which the Roman initiator would have reserved to the kings of Rome, was lost by Tullus Hostilius, who mismanaged the electrical discharge and was destroyed. Pliny relates these facts on the authority of an ancient Etruscan tradition and mentions that Numa directed his battery with success against a monster named Volta, which was ravaging the district about Rome. In reading this story, one is almost tempted to think that Volta, the discoverer, is himself a myth and that the name of Voltaic piles goes back to the days of Numa.

All Assyrian symbols connect with this science of fire, which was the great secret of the Magi; on every side we meet with the enchanter who slays the lion and controls the serpents. That lion is the celestial fire, while the serpents are the electric and magnetic currents of the earth. To this same great secret of the Magi are referable all marvels of Hermetic Magic, the extant traditions of which still bear witness that the mystery of the Great Work consists in the ruling of fire.

The learned Patricius published in his *Philosophical Magic* the Oracles of Zoroaster, collected from the works of Platonic writers—from Proclus on Theurgy, from the commentaries on the *Parmenides*, commentaries of Hermias on the *Phædrus* and from the notes of Olympiodorus on the *Philebos* and *Phaidon*.[1] These Oracles are firstly a clear and precise formulation of the doctrine here stated and secondly the prescriptions of magical ritual expressed in such terms as follow.

DEMONS AND SACRIFICES

We are taught by induction from Nature that there are incorporeal dæmons and that the germs of evil which exist in matter turn to the common good and utility. But these are mysteries which must be buried in the recesses of thought. For ever agitated and ever leaping in the atmosphere, the fire can assume a configuration like that of bodies. Let us go further and affirm the existence of a fire which abounds in images and reflections. Term it, if you will, a superabundant light which radiates, which speaks, which goes back into itself. It is the flaming courser of light, or rather it is the stalwart child who overcomes and breaks in that heavenly steed. Picture him as vested in flame and emblazoned with gold, or think of him naked as love and bearing the arrows of

[1] An English translation of the Chaldæan Oracles by Thomas Taylor, the Platonist, claims to have added fifty oracles and fragments not included in the collection of Fabricius. Mr. Mead says that the subject was never treated scientifically till the appearance of J Kroll's *De Oraculis Chaldaicis* at Breslau, in 1894.

Eros. But if thy meditation prolongeth itself, thou wilt combine all these emblems under the form of the lion. Thereafter, when things are no longer visible, when the Vault of Heaven and the expanse of the universe have dissolved, when the stars have ceased to shine and the lamp of the moon is veiled, when the earth trembles and the lightning plays around it, invoke not the visible phantom of Nature's soul, for thou must in no wise behold it until thy body has been purified by the holy ordeals. Enervators of souls, which they distract from sacred occupations, the dog-faced demons issue from the confines of matter and expose to mortal eyes the semblances of illusory bodies. Labour round the circles described by the rhombus of Hecate. Change thou nothing in the barbarous names of evocation, for they are pantheistic titles of God; they are magnetised by the devotion of multitudes and their power is ineffable. When after all the phantoms thou shalt behold the shining of that incorporeal fire, that sacred fire the darts of which penetrate in every direction through the depths of the world—hearken to the words of the fire.[1]

These astonishing sentences, which are taken from the Latin of Patricius, embody the secrets of magnetism and of things far deeper, which it has not entered into the heart of people like Du Potet and Mesmer to conceive. We find (*a*) the Astral Light described perfectly, together with its power of producing fluidic forms, of reflecting language and echoing the voice; (*b*) the will of the adept signified by the stalwart child mounted on a white horse—a symbol met with in an ancient Tarot card

---

[1] It must be understood that this summary or digest is an exceedingly free rendering, and it seems scarcely in accordance with the text on which Éliphas Lévi worked. Following the text of Kroll, Mr. Mead translates the first lines as follows: " Nature persuades us that the Daimones are pure, and things that grow from evil matter useful and good." The last lines are rendered: " But when thou dost behold the very sacred Fire with dancing radiance flashing formless through the depths of the whole world, then hearken to the Voice of Fire."

The Derivations of Magic

preserved in the *Bibliothèque Nationale;* [1] (*c*) the dangers of hallucination arising from misdirected magical works; (*d*) the *raison d'être* of enchantments accomplished by the use of barbarous names and words; (*e*) the magnetic instrument termed *rhombos,* [2] which is comparable to a child's humming top; (*f*) the term of magical practice, which is the stilling of imagination and of the senses into a state of complete somnambulism and perfect lucidity. [3]

It follows from this revelation of the ancient world that clairvoyant extasis is a voluntary and immediate application of the soul to the universal fire, or rather to that light—abounding in images—which radiates, which speaks and circulates about all objects and every sphere of the universe. This application is operated by the persistence of will liberated from the senses and fortified by a succession of tests. Herein consisted the beginning of magical initiation. Having attained the power of direct reading in the light, the adept became a seer or prophet; then, having established communication between this light and his own will, he learned to direct the former, even as the head of an arrow is set in a certain direction. He communicated at his pleasure either strife or peace to the souls of others; he established intercourse at a distance with those fellow-adepts

---

[1] See my *Key to the Tarot*, 1910, p. 32, and the cards which accompany this handbook. See also my *Pictorial Key to the Tarot*, 1911, pp. 144–147.

[2] One of the Chaldæan Oracles has the following counsel: "Labour thou around the *Strophalos* of Hecate," which Mr. G. R. S. Mead translates: "Be active (or operative) round the Hecatic spinning thing." He adds by way of commentary that *Strophalos* may sometimes mean a top. "In the Mysteries tops were included among the playthings of the young Bacchus, or Iacchus. They represented . . . the fixed stars (humming tops) and planets (whipping tops)."—*The Chaldæan Oracles,* vol. ii. pp. 17, 18.

[3] Accepting this definition of the term of occult research, we can discern after what manner it differs from the mystic term. The one, by this hypothesis, is lucidity obtained in artificial sleep which stills the senses, and the other is Divine Realisation in the spirit after the images of material things and of the mind-world have been cast out, so that the sanctified man is alone with God in the stillness.

who were his peers; and, in fine, he availed himself of
that force which is represented by the celestial lion.
Herein lies the meaning of those great Assyrian figures
which hold vanquished lions in their arms. The Astral
Light is otherwise represented by gigantic sphinxes, having
the bodies of lions and the heads of Magi. Considered
as an instrument made subject to magical power, the
Astral Light is that golden sword of Mithra used in his
immolation of the sacred bull. And it is the arrow of
Phœbus which pierced the serpent Python.

Let us now reconstruct in thought the great metro-
politan cities of Assyria, Babylon and Nineveh; let us
restore to their proper place the granite colossi; let us
formulate the massive temples, held up by elephants and
sphinxes; let us raise once more those obelisks from
which dragons look down with shining eyes and wings
outspread. Temples and palaces tower above these
wondrous piles. For ever concealed, but manifested also
for ever by the fact of their miracles, the priesthood and
the royalty, like visible divinities of earth, abide therein.
The temple is surrounded with clouds or glows with
supernatural brilliance at the will of the priests; now it
is dark in the daylight and again the night is enlightened;
the lamps of the temple spring of themselves into flame;
the gods are radiant; the thunders roll; and woe to that
impious person who may have invoked on his own head
the malediction of initiates. The temples protect the
palaces and the king's retainers do battle for the religion
of the Magi. The monarch himself is sacred; he is a
god on earth; the people lie prone as he passes; and
the maniac who would attempt to cross the threshold of
his palace falls dead immediately, by the intervention of
an invisible hand, and without stroke of mace or sword.
He is slain as if by the bolt, blasted by fire from heaven.
What religion and what power. How mighty are the
shadows of Nimrod, of Belus, of Semiramis. What can
surpass these almost fabulous cities, where such mighty

royalties were enthroned—these capitals of giants, capitals of magicians, of personalities identified by tradition with angels and still termed sons of God or princes of heaven. What mysteries have been put to sleep in these sepulchres of past nations; and are we better than children when we exalt our enlightenment and our progress, without recalling these startling memorials?

In his work on Magic,[1] M. Du Potet affirms, with a certain timidity, that it is possible to overwhelm a living being by a current of magnetic fluid. Magical power extends beyond this limit, but it is not confined within the measures of the putative magnetic fluid. The Astral Light as a whole, that element of electricity and of lightning, can be placed at the disposition of human will. What must be done, however, to acquire this formidable power? Zoroaster has just told us; we must know those mysterious laws of equilibrium which subjugate the very powers of evil to the empire of good. We must have purified our bodies by sacred trials, must have conquered the phantoms of hallucination and taken hold bodily of the light, imitating Jacob in his struggle with the angel. We must have vanquished those fantastic dogs which howl in the world of dreams. In a word, and to use the forcible expression of the Oracle, we must have heard the light speak. We are then its masters and can direct it, as Numa did, against the enemies of the Holy Mysteries. But if in the absence of perfect purity and if under the government of some animal passion, by which we are still subjected to the fatalities of tempestuous life, we proceed to this kind of work, the fire which we kindle will consume ourselves; we shall fall victims to the serpent which we unloose and shall perish like Tullus Hostilius.

[1] This was *La Magie Dévoilée*, which was circulated in great secrecy. Later on, and probably after the decease of the author, it appeared in the ordinary way, and in 1886 an English translation was announced under the editorship of Mr. J S. Farmer, but I believe that it was never published.

The History of Magic

It is not in conformity with the laws of Nature for man to be devoured by wild beasts. God has armed him with the power of resistance; his eyes can fascinate them, his voice restrain, his sign bring them to a pause. We know indeed, as a literal fact, that the most savage animals quail before a steady human glance and seem to tremble at the human voice. The explanation is that they are paralysed and awe-stricken by projections of the Astral Light. When Daniel was accused of imposture and false Magic, both he and his accusers were subjected by the king of Babylon to an ordeal of lions. Such beasts attack those only who fear them or of whom they are themselves afraid. It is utterly certain that the tiger will recede before the magnetic glance of a brave man, although the latter may be disarmed.

The Magi utilised this power and the kings of Assyria kept tigers, leopards and lions in their gardens, in a state of docility. Others were reserved in vaults beneath the temples for use in the ordeals of initiation. The symbolic bas-reliefs are the proof; they depict trials of strength between men and animals, and the adept, clothed in his priestly garb, controls the brutes by a glance of his eye and stays them with his hand. When such animals are depicted in one of the forms ascribed to the sphinx, they are doubtless symbolical, but in other representations the brute is of the natural order, and then the struggle seems to illustrate a theory of actual enchantment.

Magic is a science; to abuse is to lose it, and it is also to destroy oneself. The kings and priests of the Assyrian world were too great to be free from this danger, if ever they fell; as a fact, pride did come upon them and they did therefore fall. The great magical epoch of Chaldea is anterior to the reigns of Semiramis and Ninus. At this time religion had begun already to materialise and idolatry to prevail. The cultus of Astarte succeeded that of the heavenly Venus and royalty arrogated to itself divine attributes under the names of Baal and of Bel, or Belus. Semiramis made religion subservient to politics and conquests, replacing the old mysterious temples by ostentatious and ill-advised monuments. This notwithstanding, the magical idea continued to prevail in art and science, sealing the constructions of that epoch with the characteristics of inimitable power and grandeur. The palace of Semiramis was a building synthesis of entire Zoroastrian dogma, and we shall recur to it in explaining the symbolism of those seven masterpieces of antiquity which are called the wonders of the world.

The priesthood became secondary to the empire as the result of an attempt to materialise its own power. The fall of the one was bound to involve the other, and it came to pass under the effeminate Sardanapalus. This prince, abandoned to luxury and indolence, reduced the science of the Magi to the level of one of his courtesans. What purpose did marvels serve if they failed in ministration to pleasure? Compel, O enchanters, compel the winter to produce roses; double the savour of wine; apply your power over the light to make the beauty of women shine like that of divinities. The Magi obeyed and the king passed from intoxication to intoxication. But it came about that war was declared and that the enemy was already on the march. That enemy might signify little to the sybarite steeped in his pleasures. But it was ruin, it was infamy, it was death. Now Sardanapalus did not fear death, since for him it was an endless sleep, and he knew how to avoid the toils and humiliations of servitude. The last night came; the victor was already upon the threshold; the city could stand out no longer; the kingdom of Assyria must end on the morrow. The palace of Sardanapalus was illuminated and blazed with such splendour that it lightened all the consternated city. Amidst piles of precious stuffs, amidst jewels and golden vessels, the king held his final orgie. His women, his favourites, his accomplices, his degenerate priests surrounded him; the riot of drunkenness mingled with the music of a thousand instruments; the tame lions roared; and a smoke of perfumes, going up from the vaults of the palace, enveloped the whole edifice in a heavy cloud. But tongues of fire began to penetrate the cedar panelling; the frenzied songs were replaced by cries of terror and groans of agony. The magic which, in the hands of its degraded adepts, could not safeguard the empire of Ninus, did at least mingle its marvels to emblazon the terrible memories of this titanic suicide. A vast and sinister splendour, such as the night of Babylon had never seen, seemed suddenly to set back and enlarge the vault of heaven; a noise, like all the thunders of the world pealing together, shook the earth, and the walls of the city collapsed. Thereafter a deeper night descended; the palace of Sardanapalus melted, and when the morrow came his conqueror found no trace of its riches, no trace even of the king's body and all his luxuries.

So ended the first empire of Assyria, and the civilisation founded of old by the true Zoroaster. Thus also ended Magic, properly so called, and the reign of the Kabalah began. Abraham on coming out from Chaldea carried its mysteries with him. The people of God increased in silence, and we shall meet before long with Daniel confounding the miserable enchanters of Nebuchadnezzar and Belshazzar.[1]

[1] Éliphas Lévi adds in a note that, according to Suidas, Cedrenus and the *Chronicle of Alexandria*, it was Zoroaster himself who, seated in his palace, disappeared suddenly and by his own will, with all his secrets and all his riches, in a great peal of thunder. He explains that every king who exercised divine power passed for an incarnation of Zoroaster, and that Sardanapalus converted his pyre into an apotheosis.

Printed in the United States
139989LV00003B

9781430406822